A FINE WILL BE CHARGED FOR EACH OVERDUE BOOK

LIFE

OF

JAMES MARS

LIFE

OF

JAMES MARS,

A SLAVE

BORN AND SOLD IN

CONNECTICUT.

EIGHTH EDITION.

WRITTEN BY HIMSELF.

HARTFORD:
PRESS OF CASE, LOCKWOOD & COMPANY.
1869.

Reprinted by Mnemosyne Publishing Co., Inc. Miami, Florida

TO WHOM IT MAY CONCERN:

These will certify that the bearer, DEA. JAMES MARS, has been known to me and to the citizens of this town for a long period of years, as an honest, upright, truthful man,—a good citizen, an officer in his church, and a man whose life and character have gained the approbation, the esteem, and the good wishes of all who know him. Born a slave, the good providence of God has long since made him free, and, I trust, also taught him that "where the Spirit of the Lord is, there is liberty."

JNO. TODD.

PITTSFIELD, Mass., June 23, 1868.

First Mnemosyne reprinting 1969

**Reprinted from a copy in the
Fisk University Library Negro Collection.**

Copyright © 1969   Mnemosyne Publishing Co., Inc.   Miami, Florida

Library of Congress Catalog Card Number:

76-89394

Printed in the United States of America

INTRODUCTION.

WHEN I made up my mind to write this story, it was not to publish it, but it was at the request of my sister that lived in Africa, and has lived there more than thirty years. She had heard our parents tell about our being slaves, but she was not born until a number of years after they were free. When the war in which we have been engaged began, the thought came to her mind that her parents and brothers and sisters were once slaves, and she wrote to me from Africa for the story. I came to Norfolk on a visit at the time the war broke out, and some in Norfolk remember that I was once a slave. They asked me about it; I told them something about it; they seemed to take an interest in it, and as I was in Norfolk now, and having an opportunity to write it, I thought I would write it all through. In telling it to those, there were a great many things that I did not mention that I have written. After I had written it out, I saw that my brother and my other sister would think that I might give them the same ; and my children had often asked me to write it. When I had got it written, as it made more writing than I was willing to undertake to give each of them one, I thought I would have it printed, and perhaps I might sell enough to pay the expenses, as many of the people now on the stage of life do not know that slavery ever lived in Connecticut.

A SLAVE BORN AND SOLD IN CONNECTICUT.

THE treatment of slaves was different at the North from the South; at the North they were admitted to be a species of the human family. I was told when a slave boy, that some of the people said that slaves had no souls, and that they would never go to heaven, let them do ever so well.

My father was born in the State of New York, I think in Columbia county. He had, I think, three different masters in that State, one by the name of Vanepps, and he was Gen. Van Rensaeller's slave in the time of the Revolution, and was a soldier in that war; he was then owned by a man whose name was Rutser, and then was owned in Connecticut, in Salisbury, and then by the minister in North Canaan.

My mother was born in old Virginia, in Loudin county; I do not remember the name of the town. The minister of North Canaan, whose name was Thompson, went to Virginia for a wife, or she came to him; in some way they got together, so that they became man and wife. He removed her to Canaan, and she brought her slaves with her, and my mother was one of them. I think there were two of my mother's brothers also. The Rev. Mr. Thompson, as he was then called, bought my father, and he was married to my mother by him. Mr. Thompson ministered to the people of Canaan in holy things;

his slaves worked his farm. For a short time things went on very well; but soon the North and the South, as now, fell out; the South must rule, and after a time the North would not be ruled. The minister's wife told my father if she only had him South, where she could have at her call a half dozen men, she would have him stripped and flogged until he was cut in strings, and see if he would do as she bid him. She told him, You mind, boy, I will have you there yet, and you will get your pay for all that you have done. My father was a man of considerable muscular strength, and was not easily frightened into obedience. I have heard my mother say she has often seen her mother tied up and whipped until the blood ran across the floor in the room where she was tied and whipped.

Well, as I said, the South and the North could not agree; the South seceded and left the North; the minister's wife would not live North, and she and her husband picked up and went South, and left my father and mother in Canaan to work the farm, and they lived on the farm until I was eight years old. My mother had one child when she came from the South; I was the first she had after she was married. They had five children born in Canaan,—three died in infancy. I was born March 3d, 1790.

Mr. Thompson used to come up from Virginia and talk about our going South. He would pat me on the head and tell me what a fine boy I was. Once when he was in Canaan, he asked me if I would not like to go with him and drive the carriage for my

1*

mistress. He said if I would go he would give me twenty-five cents, or as it was then called, twenty-five coppers. I told him I wanted the money first. He gave me a quarter, and then I would not agree to go, and he put me in the oven; that I did not like, and when I got out I would not give him the money, but his business I did not yet know. He had come to sell his farm and to take us all South. My father said he would not go alive; the minister told him he must go; my father said he never would. Well, the man that had formerly ministered to the people in holy things, sold the farm, and stock, and tools, and effects, with a few exceptions. He kept a pair of horses and harness, a wagon, a bed, and a few such articles. The harness and wagon he kept to take us to the South with. After he sold his place, he took us all to a wealthy friend of his, until he had settled up all his affairs, so as to show to the world that he was an honest and upright man. He would have them think that he feared God and let alone evil; for he was born or raised in the State of New York, and had taught the people of North Canaan the way to do, as you will see, for in former days he spoke to the people from the pulpit morally, and they thought much of the man. He had taught them slavery was right, and that the Great Almighty God had sanctioned the institution, and he would practice it. He now made his arrangements to set out on his journey; the day was fixed to leave his much-loved people and home for his southern home, where he had obtained a new home and friends and acquaintances.

My father, although a slave without education, was intensely watching the movements of the teacher of the people, but kept all that he saw to himself, yet he was steadily planning his escape. The set day had now within about thirty-six hours come; all went on well with the man from the South. He had had no thought but all was well; those fine chattels were his, and would fetch him in a southern market, at a moderate estimate, two thousand dollars; they would furnish him pocket change for some time, and also his loving wife could have a chance to wreak her vengeance on my father for what she called disobedience.

It was a matter of doubt with my father what course to take,—how he could get away with his family the best and safest; whether to go to Massachusetts, which joined Canaan on the north, or to Norfolk, which joined Canaan on the east. Very fortunately for us, there was at that time an unpleasant feeling existing between the two towns or the inhabitants of Canaan and Norfolk. He said that the people of Canaan would side with their former pastor, and he found that the people of Norfolk would take sides against Canaan and their pastor; then he thought the best that he could do would be to take his family to Norfolk, where they would be the safest. He concluded to take them to Norfolk, but how was he to get them there with what he wanted to take with them? He came to the conclusion that the horses he had for a long time driven might as well help him now in this hour of distress as not. He got a colored man to help him that was stout and healthy. They hitched up the parson's team, put on board what few things he had and his family, in the still of a dark night, for it was very dark, and started for Norfolk, and on the way we run afoul of a man's wood-pile, for it was so dark he could not see the road; but we got off from the wood-pile without harm, and arrived in Norfolk about one o'clock. I think we stopped at a tavern kept by Mr. G. Pettibone, and in him we found a friend. We unloaded what we had, and father and the man that was with him took the team back to Canaan, so that the parson might set out on his journey and not have to wait for his team, and father returned to where he had left his family. He felt that he had done all for the parson that he well could, for he had taken away his family off from his hands, so that the parson would be relieved from the care that must necessarily occur in such a long journey with a family on his hands to see to, and my father thought that the parson's old Jewel would be relieved from some of her pardoned habits and from a promise she had so often made to him when she got him South. Well, how the parson felt when he had got himself out of bed, and found that he was left to pursue his journey alone, the reader can tell as well as I, for he was a big and bristle man; but I will leave him for a while, and see what is to be done with us.

It was soon known in the morning that we were in Norfolk; the first inquiry was, where will they be safe. The place was soon found. There was a man by the name of Phelps that had a house that was not occupied; it was out of the way and out of sight. After breakfast, we went to the house; it was well located; it needed some cleaning, and that my mother could do as well as the next woman. We all went to work and got it cleaned, and the next day went into it and stopped some time. Father did what work he could get out of the way, where he would not be seen, and it was necessary for him to keep out of sight, for Norfolk was the thorough-fare to Hartford. Days and weeks passed on, and we began to feel quite happy, hoping that the par-son had gone South, as we heard nothing from him. At length we heard that he said he would have the two boys at all hazards. It was thought best that the boys should be away. So one dark night we heard that the parson was coming out with his men to find the boys, for have them he would. A man that lived near to us said he would take the boys where they would be safe. His name was Cady. It was agreed on, and he went with us over a mount-ain, over rocks and logs. It was very rough and steep, and the night was so dark that we could only see when it lightened. At last we got through the woods on the top of what is called Burr Mountain. We could look down in low grounds and see logs that were laid for the road across the meadow; at every flash they could be seen, but when it did not lighten we could not see anything; we kept on,— our pilot knew the way. At last we arrived at the place. The name of the family was Tibbals. The family consisted of an old man, a middle-aged man and his wife and four children, and a very pleasant family it was. We had not been there long before it was thought best that my brother should be still more out of the way, as he was about six years older than I, which made him an object of greater search, and they were at a loss where to send him, as he was then about fourteen years of age. There was a young man by the name of Butler, from Massachusetts; he was in Norfolk at the time, studying law; he said he would take him home with him, and he did so, as I supposed, and I saw him no more for more than two years.

I stopped with the family a few days, and then went home, or what I called home. It was where my parents and sister were. I found them very lonely. I had not been home many days before our quiet was disturbed, for the parson had his hunters out to find our whereabouts. He somehow found where we were. My sister and myself were at play out at the door; we saw two men in the woods, a little from the house, coming very fast, and they came into the house. My father was not far from the house; mother was in the house. The men were Captain Phelps, the man who owned the house, and Mr. Butler, the law-student. They told us that we must now say whether we would go with the parson or not, and we must decide quick, for the parson was coming, and he would soon be on the spot, and there was no time to lose. Mother had said she was

not unwilling to go herself, if it was not for father
and the children, and the parson had made her such
promises that she was somewhat inclined to go. The
parson talked so fair to her, he beguiled her, I sup-
pose, somewhat as our first mother was beguiled in
the garden. The beguilers were both, I do not say
preachers, but they were both deceivers, and he
talked so smooth to mother that he beguiled her.
He told her if she would go to Canaan and see to
his things and pack them up for him, then if she did
not want to go, she need not. Mother talked with
father; he did not incline to go, but finally he consented. The parson ordered a wagon, and it was
soon on the spot; but where was Joseph?—he is not
here. "I want him to go with us, that we may be
all together," said the parson. Father saw what the
parson's plan was: he told him the boy was on the
way,—he could get him when we got to Canaan. I
should have said that those two men that came to
tell us that the parson was coming, hid in the barn
before the parson arrived, and were not seen by him.
They had a few words with my father while the parson went for his team. We set off for Canaan, and
in the land of Canaan we arrived that day. Where
is Joseph? Father said he would go for him the
next day in the morning, or in the day. Father
went, as the parson supposed, for Joseph. The parson was loading; mother was packing; all was now
going on well. Night came, and when all was still,
for father had told some one it would be late before
he got back, he came and took the parson's horses,

and took mother and the two children on horseback, and instead of going South, went to Norfolk, and got there about two o'clock in the morning. We stopped at a tavern kept by Captain Lawrence. The horses were sent back for the parson, for he said he should start the next day; but it seemed that he did not start for old Virginia, for we often heard of him after that day.

We stopped with Capt. Lawrence a few days. It was thought best by our friends that we should not all be together, for it was found that the parson was still in the land, and on the lookout for us. I was sent to a woman in the neighborhood, by the name of Darby—a poor woman. I stopped with her a few days, with instructions to keep still. The old lady had but one room in her house. You may wonder why I was sent to such a place; most likely it was thought she had so little room that she would not be suspected of harboring a fugitive.

A man by the name of Walter lived near by; he was in the habit of coming in to see how his boy did, as he called me. He told me when any one came there I must get under the bed. I used to sit in the corner of the room, so that I should not be seen from the window. I stayed there a number of days,—I do not now remember how many. One day I ventured to take a peep through the key-hole; the door was locked. Some one came to the door; I made a bound, and then a roll, and I was out of sight. The door was opened, and it was my friend Mr. Walter. He was quite amused to hear the performance; he said he would take me with him the next day, he was going to work in a back lot where it would be out of sight. So the next day I went with him; it was quite a treat. At noon we ate our dinner in the field; that was new to me. After dinner Mr. Walter lay down on the ground; he told me he should go to sleep, and I must keep a look-out·to see if any one came in sight. If I saw any one, I must wake him. I kept watch, but there was none came to disturb him in his repose. The day passed away, and we returned home at night—all well, as I supposed; but it seemed that the parson had his pickets out, and had got an idea that I was somewhere in the street. That night I had to leave my place at Mrs. Darby's, and went about a mile to a man's house by the name of Upson; he lived on a back street. I thought him to be a friend; I do not know but he was,—but as I find that men now act in relation to slavery, I am inclined to think otherwise. The next morning the man went to his work; he was painting for the minister in Norfolk. Mrs. Upson sent me to the brook, a little way from the house, to fetch a pail of water. I did not like going into the street very much, but being taught by my parents to obey, I went without any words. As I got to the brook, a man rode into the brook with a cocked hat on. I did not much like his looks. I did not know who he was. Said he,—"My boy, where is your father and mother?" I said, "I don't know, sir." "Where is your brother?" "I don't know, sir." "Where do you live?" "I don't know, sir." "Whom do you stay with?" "I don't know, sir." I did not then know the name of the man. He rode off, or rather I left him asking questions. He looked after me till I got to the house, and rode up. I asked Mrs. Upson who it was that came to the brook when I was there. She said it was Mr. Robbins, the minister. I thought nothing of it, for I thought all the people in Norfolk were our friends. In a few hours, the woman sent me to the neighbor's to get some water from the well. It was a widow woman where I went to get the water, and there I found my father. He said that Capt. Lawrence had been there and told him that Mr. Robbins had sent his son to Canaan to tell parson Thompson that he had seen one of his boys, and we must go in the woods, for he thought the parson would come out to look for me. Father took the water and went with it to the house that I brought the pail from. The family where I went for the water, I shall always remember with the kindest feelings. We have ever, from that day to the present, been on the best terms, and I believe three of them are living now. Two of them live in that same house that they then lived in, and the transactions of this narrative took place sixty five years ago. Their name is Curtiss.

When father came back, we set off for the woods pointed out by our friends; we went across the lots and came to a road, and crossed that into another open field. The woods were in the backside of the field. As we went on, we ascended a ridge of land, and we could see the road that led from Canaan to

Norfolk. The road then went past the burying-ground, and we could see it from where we were. We saw fourteen men on horseback; they were men we knew; the parson was one of them. We hid behind a log that was near us until they got out of sight; we then went into the woods, and there we found my mother and sister; they had been sent there by the man that had told us of the parson's information of where I was. We all remained there. This I should think was about two or three o'clock in the afternoon. Very soon the thought of night came to mind; how we were to spend the night, and what we should do for something to eat; but between sundown and dark a man passed along by the edge of the woods, whistling as he went. After he had passed on, father went up where the man went along, and came back with a pail or basket, and in it was our supper. We sat down and ate. The man we saw no more that night, but how were we to spend the night I could not tell; it was starlight, yet it was out in the woods, but father and mother were there, and that was a comfort to us children, but we soon fell asleep and forgot all our troubles, and in the morning we awoke and were still in the woods. In due time the man that passed along the night before, came again with more food for us, and then went his way; his name was Walter. We spent several days in the woods,—how many I do not remember. I think it was the fore part of the week when we went into the woods; we were there over the Sabbath, for I well remember a man by the name of Bishop had a shop where he fulled and dressed cloth not very far from where we were, and he came to the back door of his shop and stood and looked out a while, and went in and shut the door. I felt afraid he would see us. We kept very still, but I think he did not know that we were there; if he did, it did us no hurt. We were fed by kind friends all the time we were in the woods.

One afternoon, or towards night, it was thought it would be safe to go to a barn and sleep. After it was dark we went to a barn belonging to a Mr. Munger and slept, but left it while the stars were shining, and so for a few nights, and then it was thought we might sleep in the house. The next night after dark, we went in the house of Mr. Munger for the night. My sister and myself were put up in a back chamber, behind barrels and boxes, closely put together, out of sight for safe-keeping. We had not been there long before mother came and told us we must get up, for Captain Lawrence, our friend, had sent word that the parson said he would have the boys at any rate, whether he got the parents or not. His pickets were going to search every house within a mile of the meeting-house that night, or search until he found them. But we went into the woods again; we were there awhile again; when it rained, we went sometimes into a barn when we dared. After a time it was rather still, and we were at one house and sometimes at another. We had pickets out as well as the parson. It was thought best that I should not be with the rest of the family, for the hunt seemed to be for the boys. My brother, I have said, was out of the State. I was sent to one family, and then to another, not in one place long at a time. The parson began to think the task harder than he had an idea; it rather grew worse and more perplexing; he did not know what to do. He was outwitted in all his attempts; every effort or trial he had made, had failed. He now thought of giving my father and mother and sister their freedom if they would let him have the boys to take with him; this they would not do.

After some time was spent, the parson or his pickets had an idea that we were all at Capt. Lawrence's house, shut up there; how to find out if we were there or not, was the puzzle. They contrived various plans, but did not succeed. Finally there was one thing yet. They knew that Mr. Lawrence loved money; they thought they would tempt him with that; so they came to his house and made trial. They met together one day and wanted to search his house; he would not consent for a time; they urged and he refused. He finally told them on certain conditions they might go into every room but one. They went into all the rooms but one. They then wanted to go into the room that they had not been into; they offered him money to let them go into the room,— how much he did not tell, as I know of. He finally consented. The much-desired room was a chamber over the kitchen. Mr. Lawrence opened the door at the foot of the stairs, and called and said, "Jupiter! (for that was my father's first name,) you must look

2*

out for yourself now, for I can not hide you any longer." He then told the parson's pickets they must take care, for Jupiter says he will kill the first man that lays hands on him. They hesitated some; they then went up stairs still, and stopped a short time, and then with a rush against the door, it gave way, and they all went in. They found the landlady sitting there as composed as summer, with her knitting-work, unconscious of an arrest to go south as a slave! but they found us not, although the room they last went into was the one we had occupied all the time we were in that house, sometimes one night, sometimes a week, and then in the woods or elsewhere, as was thought best to keep out of the way.

The pickets returned to the land of Canaan to see what was to be the next move. The parson then proposed to give my father and mother and sister their freedom, if they would let him have the boys. That they would not do; but the boys he said he must have. As my brother was away, it was thought best that I should be away. I was sent to Mr. Pease, well-nigh Canaan, and kept rather dark. I was there for a time, and I went to stay with a man by the name of Camp, and was with him a time, and then I went to stay with a man by the name of Akins, and stayed with him a few days, and went to a man by the name of Foot, and was with him a few days. I went to another man by the name of Akins, and was there some time. The parson was not gone south yet, for he could not well give up his prey. He then proposed to sell the boys until they were twenty-five,

to somebody here that my parents would select, for
that was as long as the law of Connecticut could
hold slaves, and he would give the other members
of the family their freedom.   It was finally thought
best to do that if the purchasers that were acceptable could be found.   Some friends were on the lookout.   Finally a man by the name of Bingham was
found ; it was a man that my father was once a slave
to ; he would take my brother,—then a man by the
name of Munger would buy me if they could agree.
Mr. Bingham lived in Salisbury, Mr. Munger lived
in Norfolk ; the two men lived about fifteen miles
apart, both in Connecticut.

The trade was made, and we two boys were sold
for one hundred pounds a head, lawful money,—
yes, sold by a man, a minister of the gospel in Connecticut, the land of steady habits.   It would seem
that the parson was a worshiper with the Athenians,
as Paul said unto them when he stood on Mars Hill,
he saw an inscription on one of their altars; and it
would seem that the parson forgot or passed over
the instruction of the apostle that God made of one
blood all nations of men for to dwell on all the face
of the earth.

The parson was a tall man, standing six feet in
his boots, and had no legitimate children to be heirs
to his ill-gotten gains.   The bargain was made on
the 12th of September, 1798.   Then I was informed
that I was sold to Mr. Munger, and must go and
live with him.   The man I did not know, but the
thought of being sold, not knowing whether I was

ever to see my parents, or brother, or sister again, was more than I could endure; the thought that I was sold, as I did not then know for how long, it was hard to think of; and where were my parents I knew not: It was a sad thought, but go I must. The next morning (I was to go the morning of the 13th) was a sad morning to me. The morning was clear, without a cloud. I was told where the man lived, and I must go, for he had bought me. I thought of my parents; should I, oh! should I never see them again? As I was taught to obey my superiors, I set out; it was a little over a mile. The way was long. I went alone. Tears ran down my cheeks. I then felt for the first time that I was alone in the world, no home, no friends, and none to care for me. Tears ran, but it did no good; I must go, and on I went. And now sixty-five years have passed away since that time; those feelings are fresh in my memory. But on my way to my new home I saw my father; I will not attempt to describe my feelings when he told me he had taken rooms in the same neighborhood, and should be near me. That made the rough way smooth. I went on then cheerful and happy. I arrived at the place. I found a man with a small family; it consisted of himself and wife and three daughters. The oldest was near my age. The family appeared pleasant. I ate a bowl of bread and milk, and was told to mount a horse that was at the door with a bag of rye on his back, and ride to the field; that was about a mile off. The man went with me, and on the way we passed the house of Mrs.

Curtiss, where I mentioned in the former part of this narrative of going for well-water for Mrs. Upson. We went to the field and worked that day; went home at night. The family appeared very pleasant, and I felt pleased to think that the parson had gone, for I was told that he went the same day that I went to my new home. In a short time my father and mother and sister came into the neighborhood to live. I was allowed to go and see them one evening in two weeks. They lived about sixty rods from where I lived. Things went on well. I was very contented, and felt glad that the fear of being carried south was at an end. The parson was out of town and out of mind. I soon became acquainted with Mrs. Curtiss' boys, for I passed the house where they lived every day, as Mr. Munger's farm was beyond where they lived. I soon was feeling contented and happy. There was one thing that was unfortunate for me; Mr. Munger was not a stout, strong man, and not very healthy, and had no other help but me, and of course I had many things to do beyond my strength. I do not complain of many things, yet there are two things more I will mention. One of them I feel to this day, and that I feel the most is that I did not have an opportunity to go to school as much as I should, for all the books I ever had in school were a spelling-book, a primer, a Testament, a reading-book called Third Part, and after that a Columbian Orator. My schooling was broken and unsteady after the first and second winters, as Mr. Munger had no help, and had to go something like two miles for his wood. He would take me with him to the woods, and he would take a load and go home, and leave me to chop while he was gone. The wood was taken off from a fallow where he had sowed rye. It was in piles. Some had to be cut once, and some twice, and some three times. I went to school the most of the first winter; after that my schooling was slim. The other thing was, he was fond of using the lash. I thought so then, and made up my mind if I ever was the strongest I would pay back some of it. However, things went on, and I thought a good deal of Mr. Munger; yet I wonder sometimes why I was not more contented than I was, and then I wonder why I was as contented as I was. The summers that I was thirteen and fourteen, I was sick; they began to think I had the consumption. They sometimes would say to me, "If you should die we should lose a hundred pounds." I do not know as Mr. Munger ever said that, but it was said to me. But I will pass on with my story.

I soon found out that I was to live or stay with the man until I was twenty-five. I found that white boys who were bound out, were bound until they were twenty-one. I thought that rather strange, for those boys told me they were to have one hundred dollars when their time was out. They would say to me sometimes, "You have to work four years longer than we do, and get nothing when you have done, and we get one hundred dollars, a Bible. and two suits of clothes." This I thought of.

Some of the family or friends of the family would

tell me what a good boy I should be, because Mr. Munger saved me from slavery. They said I must call him Master; but Mr. Munger never told me to, so I never did. If he had told me to, I should have done so, for I stood greatly in fear of him, and dreaded his displeasure, for I did not like the lash. I had made up my mind that I would not stay with him after I was twenty-one, unless my brother did with the man he lived with. My brother had been home to see us, and we went once to see him. I asked my brother how long he was going to stay with Mr. Bingham. He said Mr. Bingham said he should have his time when he was twenty-one. Well then, I would have my time, I said to myself. Things went on, and I found Mr. Munger to be a very good sort of a man. I had now got to be fifteen years of age. I had got my health, and had grown to be a big boy, and was called pretty stout, as the word is, yet I was afraid of Mr. Munger. I actually stood in fear of him.

I had now got to be in my sixteenth year, when a little affair happened, which, though trivial in itself, yet was of consequence to me. It was in the season of haying, and we were going to the hayfield after a load of hay. Mr. Munger and I were in the cart, he sitting on one side and I on the other. He took the fork in both of his hands, and said to me very pleasantly, "Don't you wish you were stout enough to pull this away from me?" I looked at him, and said, "I guess I can;" but I did not think so. He held it toward me with both his hands hold of the stale. I looked at him and then at the fork, hardly daring to take hold of it, and wondering what he meant, for this was altogether new. He said, "Just now see if you can do it." I took hold of it rather reluctantly, but I shut my hand tight. I did as Samson did in the temple ; I bowed with all my might, and he came to me very suddenly. The first thought that was in my mind was, my back is safe now. All went on well for two months or more ; all was pleasant, when one day he—or Mr. Munger, I should have said—was going from home, and he told me, as was usual, what to do. I went to my work, and did it just as he told me. At night, when he came home, he asked me what I had been doing. I told him, but he did not seem satisfied. I told him I had done just what he told me. He said I had not done what I ought to have done. I told him I had done what he told me. That was more than I had ever said before. He was angry and got his horsewhip, and said he would learn me. He raised his hand and stood ready to strike. I said, "You had better not!" I then went out at the door. I felt grieved to see him in such a rage when I had done just as he told me, and I could not account for it. If he had been a drinking man, I should not have wondered; but he was not, he was a sober man. I could not get over my feeling for some time, but all was pleasant the next day. I said to his daughters that I would not stay there a day after I was twenty-one, for I did not know what their father meant. I did just as he told me, and thought I was doing what he would be satisfied with. They told me not to mind it. Things went on from that time as well as I could wish. From that time until I was twenty-one, I do not remember that he ever gave me an unpleasant word or look. While I lived with him, after that time, I felt that I had now got as good a place as any of the boys that were living out. I often went with his team to Hartford and to Hudson, which the other boys did not that lived in the neighborhood. I now felt that I could do anything for the family; I was contented and happy.

The year that I was eighteen, Mr. Munger was concerned in an iron establishment, manufacturing iron. He had a sister living in Oneida county, and he learned that iron was high or brought a good price there. He told me he thought he would send a load out there and get a load of wheat, and asked me if I would go out with a load. I told him I would if he wished me to; he said he did. He got every thing ready, and I set out the 17th day of October, and thought it would take me about two weeks or thereabouts. On I went, and when I got there I could exchange my iron for wheat readily, but none had their wheat out, and their barn-floors were so full that they could not thrash. I had to wait a week. As soon as I got my load, I set out for home. I was gone a day or two over three weeks. After I got to Norfolk, I passed the house where my parents lived. They told me that it was very current with the people that I had sold the

3

horses and wagon, and was seen by some one that knew me, and was on my way to Canada. They said that Mr. Munger said he did not believe it,— he said he should not trouble himself. Yet I went on home. He was glad to see me; asked if I had any bad luck. I told how it was, and he was satisfied, and said when he saw the team that they were in better condition than they were when I left home. "Now they may talk as much as they please; you and the team, wagon and load are here." And when I told him what I had done, he said he was perfectly satisfied, I had done well; he had no fault to find. Every thing went on first-rate. I did my best to please him, and it seemed to me that the family did the same. I now took the hardest end of the work. I was willing to do what I could. I was willing to work, and thought much of the family, and they thought something of me. Mr. Munger was receiving his share of offices of the town, and was from home a portion of his time. I felt ambitious to have our work even with others. He said his work went on as well as if he was there.

When I was in my twentieth year, a nephew of Mr. Munger came to board with him; he was studying law. Mr. Munger and I were accustomed to talk about my term of service with him. I told him I did not mean to stay with him until I was twenty-five. He said he thought I would if I meant to do what was fair and just. I told him that my brother had his time when he was twenty-one, and I wanted my time. He finally had some talk with his nephew,

who said that he could hold me. But finally Mr.
Munger made me an offer of what he would give me
if I would stay. I thought the offer was tolerably
fair. I had now become attached to the family. I
told him that I would stay, as he had often said he
thought I ought to stay after I was twenty-one. I
thought I would divide the time with him in part,
as the offer he made would not cover the whole time.
All was fixed, and I worked on. Nothing more was
said for a long time about it; then the thing was
spoken about, and the same mind was in us both,
and I felt satisfied. The fall previous to my being
twenty-one came; all was right, as I thought. The
winter came and nothing was said. The last of Feb-
ruary came. I heard it hinted that Mr. Munger had
said that he should not make any bargain with me,
but if I left him he would follow me. The thing
was understood by us, and I paid no attention to it.
March came, and nothing was said. The third of
March was my birthday. All was quiet, and I kept
on as before until the first of April. It was told me
that Mr. Munger said that his nephew had examined
the law and found that he could hold me, and what
he gave me would be his unless he was bound by a
written agreement. As there were no writings given,
I began to think it was time to know how it was.
There was another thing now came to mind.

When I was thirteen years old, Mr. Munger bought
a calf of my father, and gave it to me, and said he
would keep it until it was two years old, and then I
might sell it and have what it brought. He kept it.

He had a mate for it, and when the steers were two
years old he sold them for twenty-four dollars. He
then told me that he would give me a heifer of the
age the steer was, and when she had a calf he would
take her to double in four years. When I was sev-
enteen he gave me a heifer, and she had a calf that
spring, and the first of April he said he would take
her, and at the end of four years from that time he
would give me two cows and two calves. That was
agreed on. The next year, in March or April, one
of his oxen hooked my cow; it hurt her so that the
cow died. Well, now, what was to be done? He
said at the time agreed on I should have my cows.
I was content with that and worked on, feeling that
all would be made right. I thought I should have
two cows with those calves when I was twenty-one,
and that would be a beginning. Afterward I agreed
to stay with him until I was twenty-five; I could let
them until that time. I will now go on with my
story. I asked him for my cows and calves. He
said he should not let me have any. He said if I
stayed and did well perhaps he would give me a cow.
I asked him if that was all that I was to have if I
stayed until I was twenty-five. He said he would
see. I asked when he would see. He said when the
time came. I then told him I had been told that
Warren (that was the name of his nephew) had told
him not to give me what he had agreed to, and I
wanted to know if he would do as he had agreed to
or not. He said I belonged to him, and I could not
help myself. I told him I would stay with him as I

had said if he would give me a writing obligating himself to give me the sum we had agreed upon. After hesitating a short time, he said he would not give a writing; he would not be bound. I told him I had got that impression, "and if you say you will not give me what you said you would, I will not work another day." He then said if I left him he would put me in jail and keep me there a year at any rate. This was on Saturday. The next day I picked up what few duds I had, and at evening, as it was the Sabbath, I told him I had done all the work for him that I should do. I then bade him good night and left his house, and went to my father's. The next day in the afternoon, Mr. Munger and nephew came to my father's with a sheriff. I was not in the house. He told my father that he would pay my board in jail for one year, and I could not help myself. They took what few clothes I had, and went away before I got home. It was well it was so. I told my father that I would stay in jail as long as Mr. Munger would find money. I sent the word to Mr. Munger. He sent me word that I should have an opportunity to. My people wanted to have me go away for a time. I thought at first I would. Then I saw that I had nothing to go with, and had no clothes for a change. I would not leave. I told them I would go to jail. I thought perhaps I could get the liberty of the yard, and then I could earn something to get some clothes, and then I would leave for Canada or some other parts.

A few days after, I heard that Mr. Munger said
3*

he would leave it to men how it should be settled, and he sent me such word. I sent word to him, no, I was going to jail, if he would keep his word. He finally said as I had always been faithful, he would not or had rather not put me in jail. My parents said so much, they did not want to have me go to jail, that I finally said I would leave it to three men if they were men that I liked: if they were not, I would not. He said I might name the men; their judgment was to be final. The men were selected, the time and place specified. The day came, the parties met, and the men were on hand. Mr. Munger had his nephew for counsel; I plead my case myself. A number of the neighbors were present. Mr. Munger's counsel began by saying that his uncle had bought me, and had paid for me until I was twenty-five, and that he had a right to me. I then told his nephew that I would have a right to him some day, for he was the cause of all the difficulty. He said no more. The arbitrators asked Mr. Munger if he had anything against me. He said he had not. They asked him, in case they gave him anything, if he wished me to work it out with him; he said he did. They went out a few moments, and returned and said that I must pay Mr. Munger $90. He then asked me to go home with him, and he would hire me. I told him I would go and get my clothes, for that was in the decision. He said I could have them. His nephew did not want me to live with his uncle, if he boarded with him. I told Mr. Munger that I would not work for him. I hired

to another man, and went to work in the same neighborhood. This nephew kept an eye on me for a long
time, and always gave me the road whenever he saw
me coming. Mr. Munger and family always treated
me with attention whenever I met them; they made
me welcome to their house and to their table. If
that nephew had not interfered, there would have
been no trouble.

Things all went on pleasantly. In about four years
I went there again to work, and in a short time Mr.
Munger and his two daughters joined the church of
which his wife was a member. I joined the same
church, and was often at his house. Mr. Munger
was unfortunate and lost his property, not as people
lose their property now. He was poor and not very
healthy, and his wife and the daughter that was not
married, not being healthy, and he being a man
advanced in life, it wore upon him and his family,
and his daughter went into a decline. I went west,
and was gone about three months, and on my re-
turn went to see the family, and found the daughter
very much out of health and wasting away. I called
again the next day but one. As I had been accustomed to take care of the sick, she asked me to stop
with her that night. I did so, and went to my work
in the morning. The second day after, I called again
to see her, and she made the same request. I staid
and watched with her that night. She asked what I
thought of her; I told her I feared she would never
be any better. She then asked me to stay with her
if she did not get any better, while she lived. I told

her I would. A cousin of hers, a young lady, was there, and we took the care of her for four weeks. I mention this because it was a time to be remembered and cherished by me while I live. We were in the daily habit of speaking of her prospects and how she felt. She would speak of death with as much apparent composure as of any other subject. She said very little to her friends about her feelings. The day that she died was the evening of the Sabbath. About six o'clock in the afternoon, or rather all that day, she did not appear to be as well; but at the time just mentioned she sunk away and seemed to be gone for a short time, when she revived as one out of sleep, suddenly, and seemed surprised, and said, "There is nothing that I want to stay here for; let me go." She then bade her friends farewell, and told them not to weep for her, for she was going. Her countenance seemed as if lit up with heavenly love, and for a short time she seemed to be away from the world, and then was still and said but little. About eleven o'clock she wanted to be moved. She was moved. She then wanted to drink. I gave her, or put the glass to her lips. She did not swallow any. I saw there was a change, and before her friends could get into the room her spirit had fled.

That was a scene that I love to think of. It makes me almost forget that I ever was a slave to her fa ther; but so it was. I staid until she was buried, and then I went West again. Her parents were broken-hearted indeed. I returned from the West, and spent a part of the summer with Mr. Munger.

I afterwards worked where I chose for a few years. I was frequently at Mr. Munger's house. He seemed depressed, his health rather declined, and he finally sank down and was sick. He sent for me; I went to him, and he said he wished to have me stay with him. I told him I would, and I staid with him until he died, and closed the eyes of his daughter when she died, and his also. And now to look back on the whole transaction, it all seems like a dream. It is all past, never to be re-acted. [That family have all gone, with one exception.]

APPENDIX.

This Appendix is by request of those that have read what is before it:—

After the death of Mr. Munger, I married a wife and lived in Norfolk a few years; we had two children. We went to Hartford after a while; I worked for the then known firm of E. & R. Terry. There was a man came to Hartford from Savannah, with his family; he came to school his daughter. He brought a slave girl with him to care for the smaller children. My wife washed for the family. All went on well for about two years. The Southern man's name was Bullock, and the slave's name was Nancy. One day when I was at work in the store, a gentleman came where I was; he asked if this was deacon Mars. I said "Yes, sir." He said Mr. Bullock was about to send Nancy to Savannah, "and we want to make a strike for her liberty, and we want some man

to sign a petition for a writ of habeas corpus to bring
Mr. Bullock before Judge Williams; they tell me
that you are the man to sign the petition." I asked
him who was to draw the writ; he said Mr. Wm. W.
Ellsworth. I went to Mr. Ellsworth's office with the
man. I signed the petition. I then went to my
work. I told Mr. Ellsworth that it would cause an
excitement; if he wanted me at any time, I would
be on hand. The writ was served on Mr. Bullock, and
he was brought before Judge Williams, but Nancy
could not be found. The court adjourned till eight
o'clock the next morning. At night Nancy came to
the house where they were boarding; she had been
out as she was accustomed to go with the children.
Mrs. Bullock told Nancy to go to bed. She somehow had an idea that all was not right; she opened
the door, and gave it a swing to shut, but it did not
shut, as she said afterwards. She thought she would
see what they were talking about. She said Mrs. B.
told Mr. Bullock to start in the morning at 4 o'clock
with Nancy for New York; "never mind the bond,
and send Nancy South." I omitted to mention that
the court put Mr. Bullock under a bond of $400 to
appear the next morning at 8 o'clock. The plan to
send Nancy South was fixed on. Nancy said to herself, "When you come where I be, I wont be there."
She went out of the house, and went to the house of
a colored man and stopped for the night. The next
morning the court sat; master and slave were both
there. The court said it was the first case of the
kind ever tried in the State of Connecticut, and the

Supreme Court of Errors was to meet in ten days,
and was composed of five judges; he would adjourn.
the trial until the session of that court.

During those ten days I had a fair opportunity to
see how strong a hold slavery had on the feelings of
the people in Hartford. I was frowned upon; I was
blamed; I was told that I had done wrong; the house
where I lived would be pulled down; I should be
mobbed; and all kinds of scarecrows were talked
about, and this by men of wealth and standing. I
kept on about my work, not much alarmed. The
ten days passed away; the Supreme Court of Errors
sat; Judge Williams was chief judge. The case was
argued on both sides. When the plea was ended,
then came the decision:—two of the court would
send Nancy back to slavery; two were for her re-
lease; we shall hear from Williams to-morrow at
eight o'clock.

At the time appointed all were in attendance to
hear from Judge Williams. The Judge said that
slavery was tolerated in some of the States, but it
was not now in this State; we all liked to be free.
This girl would like to be free; he said she should
be free,—the law of the State made her free, when
brought here by her master. This made a change
in the feelings of the people. I could pass along the
streets in quiet. Nancy said when she went into the
court-house on the last day she had two large pills
of opium; had she been sentenced to go back, she
should have swallowed both of them before she left
the court-house.

Now to my family. I have said I had two children born in Norfolk, and six in Hartford. One died in infancy. I lived in Hartford about sixteen years. I took a very prominent part in the organization of the Talcott Street Church. I moved from Hartford to Pittsfield, Mass. When I had been there three years and a half, my wife died in November; the May following I lost a son sixteen years of age. My oldest son enlisted in the U. S. Navy when he was eighteen, and has followed the sea ever since. I had another that went to sea, that I have not heard from for eight years. My oldest daughter went to Africa, to Cape Palmas; she went out a teacher, and has been there five years. I have one son who, when the war broke out, when the first gun was fired on Sumter, wanted to enlist, and did enlist in the navy, and went out on the brig Bainbridge, and served until she was stopped for repairs. He then went on the Newbern and served his time, and has an honorable discharge. Another, and the last one, enlisted in the artillery and went to New Orleans, but never, no, never came back, nor will he ever come again. I have a daughter in Massachusetts, of a frail constitution. She has a family to care for. I have none to care for me that has anything to spare, yet my children are willing to help as far as they are able. As they are not able I feel willing to do all that I can to help to get my living. The question is sometimes asked me if I have not any means of support. The fact is, I have nothing but what I have saved within the last three years. I have spent a portion of that time with my book about the country. I am now in my eightieth year of age, I cannot labor but little, and finding the public have a desire to know something of what slavery was in the State of Connecticut, in its time, and how long since it was at an end, in what year it was done away, and believing that I have stated the facts, many are willing to purchase the book to satisfy themselves as to slavery in Connecticut. Some told me that they did not know that slavery was ever allowed in Connecticut, and some affirm that it never did exist in the State. What I have written of my own history, seems to satisfy the minds of those that read it, that the so called, favored state, the land of good morals and steady habits, was ever a slave state, and that slaves were driven through the streets tied or fastened together for market. This seems to surprise some that I meet, but it was true. I have it from reliable authority. Yes, this was done in Connecticut.

August 22d, 1866, I had a fall and uncapped my knee, that laid me by ten months, so that I was unable to travel or do anything to help myself, but by the help of Him that does all things well, I have got so as to be able to walk with a staff. During the time that I was confined with my knee, I met with kind treatment, although I was away from home. I was in the state of New York at the time of my misfortune, away from any of my relations, still I was under the watchful care of a Friend that sticketh closer than a brother. He has thus far provided for me, and I feel assured that He will if I trust Him, with all my heart and soul and strength, and serve Him faithfully, which is my duty, the few years or days that are allotted to me, and it is my prayer that I may have grace to keep me, that I may not dishonor the cause of Christ, but that I may do that which will be acceptable in the sight of my Heavenly Father, so that I may do good to my fellow-men.

One thing in my history I have not mentioned, which I think of importance. Although born and raised in Connecticut, yes, and lived in Connecticut more than three-fourths of my life, it has been my privilege to vote at five Presidential elections. Twice it was my privilege and pleasure to help elect the lamented and murdered Lincoln. I am often asked when slavery was abolished in Connecticut; my answer is, the Legislature in 1788, passed an act that freed all that were born after 1792, those born before that time that were able to take care of themselves, must serve until they were twenty-five; my time of slavery expired in 1815. Connecticut I love thy name, but not thy restrictions. I think the time is not far distant when the colored man will have his rights in Connecticut.